COURT LORD

Who Controlled the Court Better,

Bill Russell or Wilt Chamberlain

Raphael R. Wilson

Table Of Contents

Table Of Contents   **2**

Chapter One   **3**
The Goated: A Visionary Man   3
Faced Prejudice   10

Chapter Two   **21**
Another Day in the Court   21
The Court Wizard: Bill Russell vs Wilt Chamberlain   23
Upping the Ante   26

Chapter Three   **42**
Legacy of Bill Russell   43
The Victory in the End   44
Unknown Person in Alcatraz   46
The NBA Founding Father   50

End Notes   **55**

Chapter One

The Goated: A Visionary Man

Bill Russell amassed a history of championship accomplishments during his basketball career that is unmatched in any sport. He led the Boston Celtics to 11 NBA titles over the next 13 years while serving as the premier defensive player of his age, helping the United States basketball team win an Olympic gold medal in 1956.

During the franchise's heyday in the 1950s and 1960s, Mr. Russell established himself as the most successful athlete in team sports history, earning him eternal fame. He became the first Black man to occupy that position in a major American professional sport when the Celtics selected him as head coach in 1966.

Mr. Russell, who passed away on July 31 at the age of 88, was one of the most interesting public characters to cross athletics and civil rights. He was unflappable on and off the court. He was a highly motivated and creative athlete, especially when matched up against Wilt Chamberlain, the era's greatest scorer, in enthralling contests. The popularity of the National Basketball Association increased as a result of their rivalry.

The goateed, broad-shouldered Mr. Russell, who stood 6 feet 9 inches tall, weighed 220 pounds of lean muscle in his prime. He was quick and nimble, had a powerful vertical jump, and could stop shots with his arm extended like a bowsprit thanks to his 7-foot-4 wingspan. He transformed basketball defense by using his athleticism to block shots and grab rebounds.

Mr. Russell's intellectual interest in other facets of the game, such as shot trajectory, rebounding angles, human psychology, and gamesmanship, matched his athletic skills. He was well-known for his on-court trash talking, aggressive shot blocking, player research, and teasing of rivals. He once said that although he was aware that he couldn't stop every shot, a few solid blocks were more than enough to make his opponent unprepared.

According to writer Frank Deford's 1999 article in Sports Illustrated, "Bill Russell and the Boston Celtics teams he coached stand alone as the ultimate champions," which is the only thing we know for sure regarding excellence in sports in the United States of America in the 20th century.

While his skill as a player was being praised, Mr. Russell also had to deal with the lingering issues of racism and segregation. He was regarded as being quiet, contemplative, prickly, and principled. He was a guy who sought methods for his children to grow up "as we could not... equal... and understanding," as he once wrote in the preface to a book. He was born in the Jim Crow South.

He charged the NBA with utilizing a quota system to control the proportion of Black players in each club as early as 1958. While participating in civil rights marches with the Rev. Martin Luther King Jr., he questioned the movement's nonviolent approach, contending that African Americans had a right to self-defense.

Following the murder of civil rights activist Medgar Evers in Jackson, Mississippi, in 1963, Mr. Russell agreed to Charles

Evers' offer to conduct a youth basketball camp in Jackson that would unite Black and White kids. Despite receiving death threats, he stood by his opinions.

1960s Bill Russell Russell, who passed away on July 31 at the age of 88, served as the cornerstone of the Boston Celtics dynasty, which won 11 championships in 13 seasons. (AP) Some of Mr. Russell's admirers in Boston, which had a long history of racism, didn't like him because of his hard exterior and blunt speaking style. The Boston Red Sox baseball club didn't become integrated until 1959, and the 1970s school integration demonstrations in Boston were some of the bloodiest in the nation.

Because Mr. Russell for many years declined to sign autographs in favor of a handshake and discussion, many admirers believed him to be distant. In his 1979 book

"Second Wind: Memoirs of an Opinionated Man," he called

Boston a "flea market of prejudice."

Despite his success with the Celtics—who had never won a

championship before he joined the team—Mr. Russell did not

gain local business sponsorships and was turned down by

affluent areas when he tried to purchase a home. His

suburban Boston house was burglar into and looted in 1968.

On the walls were racial slurs, and his bed had excrement on

it.

In "Second Wind," he said, "It had all types, new and old, and

in their most virulent form." "The city had brick-throwing,

send-'em-back-to-Africa racists, crooked city hall cronies,

and false radical-chic racists in the university sections. Apart

from that, I enjoyed the city.

In 1975, he declined to attend his induction into the Naismith Memorial Basketball Hall of Fame because he objected to becoming the first African American player to be inducted. In 1972, he refused to approve a public ceremony to retire his Celtics uniform.

Mr. Russell famously stated, "We naively lionize athletes and make them heroes because they can hit a ball or catch one." Only sportsmen like [Muhammad] Ali, who we can appreciate for who they are and not just their accidental physical prowess, should we bother giving any special attention.

Mr. Russell received the Presidential Medal of Freedom, the nation's highest civilian honor, from President Barack Obama in 2010 for his achievements in athletics and his support of human rights.

Faced Prejudice

On February 12, 1934, William Felton Russell was born in Monroe, Louisiana, and his father was a worker at a paper bag plant. His recollections of his youth are rife with painful examples of bigotry, including everyday slights and overt threats against his mother and father.

His family relocated to Oakland, California when he was 9 years old to escape the systematic segregation of the South. His dad got a job at a factory that makes weapons for war. According to Mr. Russell, Louisiana is hell on earth compared to Oakland's public housing developments, which are harsh and hazardous.

His mother passed away a few years after his parents divorced. He relied on his elder brother Charlie Russell Jr., a dramatist, for assistance during their formative years.

Mr. Russell attempted organized basketball for the first time in junior high school but didn't make the squad since he was tall and clumsy as a young man. Later, only a compassionate coach could get him a position on his high school's junior varsity squad. He was probably saved from the inner city's dangerous streets by a change of circumstances. He later said, "All my energy and frustrations would have been taken in some other way if I hadn't had basketball."

Only one scholarship offer for college was made to Mr. Russell, and it came from the University of San Francisco, a little Jesuit institution without a distinguished athletics program. In 1955 and 1956, Mr. Russell guided the USF Dons to back-to-back NCAA titles and was named to the first team of all-Americans in both seasons. K.C. Jones, another of his college buddies, joined him on the Celtics and went on to have a Hall of Fame career of his own.

In addition to being a basketball superstar, Mr. Russell was also one of the best high jumpers in the nation in the 1950s.

Despite Mr. Russell's success in amateur competition, several NBA scouts were still unsure of the worth of a center who prioritized defense. Mr. Russell never put up the kind of large numbers on the scoreboard that was desired at the time from centers.

Red Auerbach, the coach of the Celtics, had no such reservations. Seeing how Mr. Russell's playing style may benefit the team's roster of future Hall of Famers, such as

Bob Cousy, Bill Sharman, and Frank Ramsey, he negotiated a trade to obtain the draft rights to Mr. Russell in 1956.

Russell swiftly seized a position in the Celtics lineup after missing almost half of his rookie season while helping the American basketball team win a gold medal at the Olympics. He then assisted the club in winning its first NBA title in 1957.

In his second season, Mr. Russell missed the Celtics' loss to the St. Louis Hawks in the NBA Finals due to an ankle ailment. Boston won two additional championships in 1967–68 and 1968–69 when Mr. Russell took over as player-coach and became the first Black head coach in major professional sports. This came after Boston had won eight straight championships under Auerbach.

None of the victories were straightforward. Mr. Russell was such a fierce competitor that he puked before every game in the locker room. He stunned spectators by almost shutting down the offensive of the other teams when he entered the floor.

He would sometimes purposefully allow a player to drive through him for what seemed to be an easy layup while he was defending that guy with the ball, recover in time to pivot, and swat the ball away from behind.

Other times, Mr. Russell would block shots repeatedly within a single possession, as if he were competing in a volleyball match against himself. He often made a quick left-handed pass to one of his teammates who was speeding down the hardwood parquet flooring at Boston Garden on a fast break after he grabbed a defensive rebound.

The rivalry between the two, who were close friends before Chamberlain joined the NBA in 1959, quickly rose to the top of the league. Although Chamberlain had higher individual stats, Mr. Russell's side ended up winning the majority of the games.

During Mr. Russell's 13 years with the Celtics, Chamberlain only participated in one NBA championship squad (the 1966–1967 Philadelphia 76ers).

In a 1997 television interview with Bob Costas, Mr. Russell stated of Chamberlain, "If he scored 62 [points] and we won, it wouldn't mean anything." But it upset me if he scored 62 and won the game.

In celebration with Boston Celtics coach Red Auerbach after the team beat the Los Angeles Lakers, 95-93, to win their eighth consecutive NBA title in 1966, Bill Russell clutches a bouquet that was sent to the locker room.

Russell averaged 15.1 points per game throughout his professional career, with 14,522 points and 21,620 rebounds. His 22.5 rebounds per game average are second only to Chamberlain's 22.9 rebounds per game average in NBA history.

Although the NBA didn't start keeping track of blocked shots as an official statistic until 1973, after Mr. Russell had retired, he also set the bar for shot-blocking.

Mr. Russell played in 12 NBA All-Star Games, won five championships for rebounds, and was five times awarded the league's most valuable player. He won the title of "the best player in the history of the NBA" in 1980, according to the nation's basketball writers.

On 1969, Mr. Russell gave up playing basketball. He then drove his automobile across the nation and made his home in Mercer Island, Washington. After some time alone, he worked as an NBA broadcast analyst for networks and appeared in a few movies and TV programs before getting back into basketball in 1973 as a coach and general manager of the Seattle SuperSonics. He held this position from 1973 to 1977. In 1987, he served as the Sacramento Kings' coach, and from 1989 to 1990, he served as the team's vice president of basketball operations.

His marriages to Dorothy Anstett and Rose Swisher, his undergraduate sweetheart, both ended in divorce. Marilyn

Nault, his third wife, passed away in 2009. Three of his children from his previous marriage, William, Karen, and Jacob, are still alive.

Mr. Russell made multiple visits back to Boston, notably for a 1999 ceremony when the Celtics re-retired his No. 6. This was a hint that things between Mr. Russell and Boston were starting to get better. At other events, he made public appearances in front of standing ovations with former teammates, including Sam Jones, John Havlicek, and Tom Heinsohn, to commemorate the occasions of their championship wins.

At Boston's City Hall Plaza, a monument of Mr. Russell was unveiled in 2013. He only consented to the monument when the local council promised to provide a grant to support a mentorship program for young people. The monument portrays Mr. Russell as the quintessential selfless teammate, knees bent and ball in hands, ready to make a chest pass. Mr. Russell is quoted as saying, "The most significant gauge of how terrific a game I'd played was how much better I'd made my teammates play," on the stone.

Chapter Two

Another Day in the Court

Bill Russell is the greatest champion in the history of basketball. Russell, the defensive anchor, and star of the 1960s Boston Celtics dynasty passed away on Sunday at the age of 88. During his career, he won 11 NBA championships, two NCAA crowns, and an Olympic gold medal.

Here is a look at the stats that led to Russell's induction into the Basketball Hall of Fame, his clashes with fellow star Wilt Chamberlain, and how Russell changed the way the defense was played in the NBA.

Russell was selected by the Celtics in the 1956 NBA Draft out of San Francisco, and they went on to form a dynasty around the rangy center that dominated the game until his retirement in 1969.

Russell once remarked, "Success is the consequence of consistently using successful techniques and strategies. "The procedure is not extraordinary in any way. There is no element of chance."

Russell's Resume Highlights

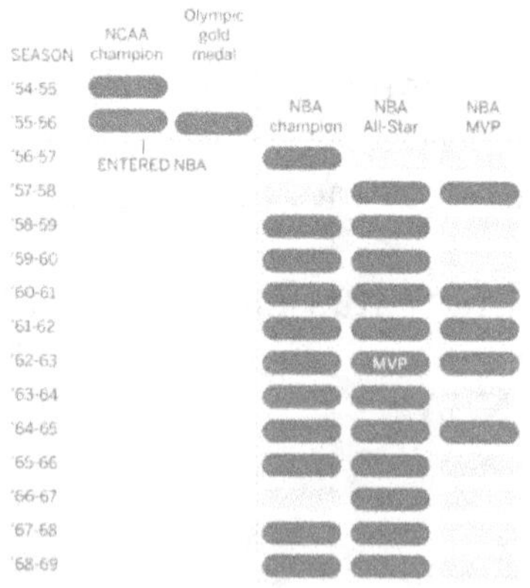

Source: www.espn.com/nba

Professional Title Won Most

11	BILL RUSSELL	Celtics
	HENRI RICHARD	Canadiens
10	YOGI BERRA	Yankees
	SAM JONES	Celtics
	YVAN COURNOYER	Canadiens
9	TOM HEINSOHN	Celtics
	KC JONES	Celtics
	SATCH SANDERS	Celtics
	JOHN HAVLICEK	Celtics
	BILL DICKEY	Yankees
	PHIL RIZZUTO	Yankees
	FRANK CROSETTI	Yankees
	LOU GEHRIG	Yankees
	RED KELLY	Maple Leafs/Red Wings
	JACQUES LEMARIE	Canadiens
	MAURICE RICHARD	Canadiens
8	JOE DIMAGGIO	Yankees
	CLAUDE PROVOST	Canadiens

The Court Wizard: Bill Russell vs Wilt Chamberlain

For the 1959–60 NBA season, Wilt Chamberlain made his debut, and he and Bill Russell began their legendary 10-year rivalry. Russell's Celtics outscored Wilt Chamberlain's squad 86-57 throughout the regular season and the playoffs for a winning percentage of.600.

The Celtics had to play us 11 to 13 times during the regular season, according to Chamberlain. "If you still don't believe that was enough, we played them again in the playoffs if it went to seven games. As a result, I had a lot more opportunities than I had intended to visit William Felton Russell."

Comparative statistics

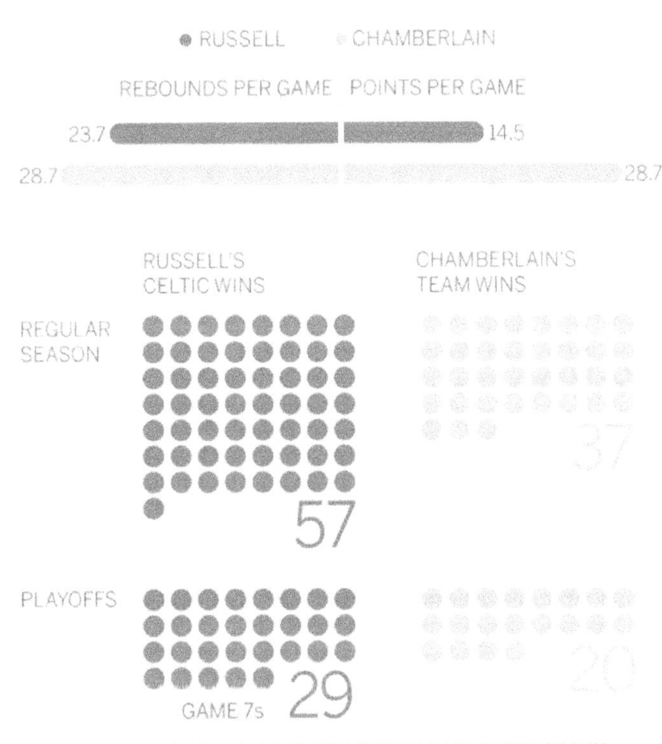

source://www.espn.com

Red Auerbach, a former Celtics head coach and current team president, said it best: "Russell single-handedly transformed this game just by emphasizing defense."

Russell had a major offensive contribution, but his reputation was built on his defense. In 11 of his 13 seasons, he was the league's defensive win share leader, including 10 consecutive from 1958 through 1967. No other player has led the NBA in this area more than five times, so that number is quite amazing (and only George Mikan and Tim Duncan did so).

Upping the Ante

Russell was always a great player, but in the playoffs, the stakes were higher, and he managed to play even better. Here is a summary of his career stats, including any changes from the regular season to the postseason:

Key figures

3.6	Russell's assist rate per 36 minutes. Despite not being as well-known for his passing as he is for other aspects of his game, he ranks third among centers in the Hall of Fame with that number, behind only Bill Walton (4.3) and Wes Unseld (3.8).
5	seasons during which Russell shared the league MVP award with Michael Jordan, placing him joint-second all-time. With six MVP seasons, Kareem Abdul-Jabbar surpasses them all.

8	athletes who have won an NBA championship, an Olympic gold medal, and an NCAA championship, includes Russell.
22.45	Rebounds per game in the regular season, second only to Chamberlain in history (22.89). Russell leads all time list for postseason rebounding average with 24.87 rebounds per game.
133.6	Russell has the highest defensive win shares overall of any player. Tim Duncan (106.3), Kareem Abdul-Jabbar (94.5), Hakeem Olajuwon (94.5), and Chamberlain are in his wake (93.9).

We live in a society that naturally reduces everything to who was the finest, most, least, or greatest. In our culture of loudness, which is dominated by television, social media, and the internet, learning is not often seen as a component of entertainment. Not for listening, ears. It's for spectacles.

The passing of Boston Celtics legend Bill Russell comes at a time when even professionals — perhaps, particularly professionals — are paid for their ability to impersonate fan partisans. In this warring culture, where argument and loudness pass for knowledge and insight. In recent weeks, ESPN commentator J.J. Redick has claimed that Bob Cousy used to be protected by "plumbers and firefighters" while he was playing in the NBA.

Draymond Green, a power forward for the Golden State Warriors, said that the 1998 Chicago Bulls of Michael Jordan could not have competed with the 2017 Warriors. Both Jerry West, 84, and Bob Cousy, 93, responded sharply to save their time. West chided Redick for being a one-dimensional player who was never a star, while Cousy made a joke about how, if true, the NBA must have had the greatest plumbers and firefighters around.

Redick made a slam on the veterans. The veterans responded with a dunk. This is the way we speak.

Professional respect, as well as a disregard for the accomplishments of earlier generations and their struggles and situations in favor of clapbacks, are casualties of this particular type of noise. It is a determined belief rather than just a performance for attention. With Russell's departure, the rhetoric will come to a brief halt, and there will be calm respect for his dignity and impressive achievements as well as the bittersweet passage of time. The lone member of the 1957 Celtics squad that won the title is Cousy. Bill Sharman has left us. Like Tommy Heinsohn, who passed away in 1969, only a select few people still exist today, like Don Chaney, Don Nelson, and Emmette Bryant.

The Black community in Boston will lament the loss of their champion—a player and a neighborhood appreciative of one another in a tough environment. Russell catalyzed for the city's Black residents to embrace the Celtics, a legacy that was overshadowed by the racist school desegregation laws of the 1970s and the divisive Larry Bird period of the 1980s, during which the Celtics came to represent whiteness. Russell selected Dennis Johnson with the Seattle SuperSonics in the 1977 draft; he passed away in 2007. 2018 will see Jo Jo White. Jones passed away in 2020. In 2021, Sam Jones died.

Respect, reverence, and understanding need to be a constant part of our conversation, but it won't be long before experts and laypeople alike resume generating lists and arguing over them. Since Russell only scored 15.1 points per game on average during his career and only shot 44 percent from the field at that time, the discussions will go up again without his being mentioned since there were so many missed shots. He did, however, average 22.5 rebounds per game.

Even Russell's greatest on-court achievement—winning 11 NBA championships in the course of a 13-year career—is constantly under attack by claims that because there were only eight NBA teams at the time Russell won all those titles, they were somehow less legitimate than championships won today because the postseason wasn't as protracted as it is now.

Russell himself is what renders these efforts at reduction ineffective because, when the noise dies down and the listening begins, the embarrassing futility of judging Bill Russell without acknowledging the fundamental fact of his existence—that he was born a Black man in the United States in 1934—neuters the numbers and metrics.

Millions of individuals, hundreds of pros, and dozens of legends share this straightforward and fundamental quality, but Russell stood out due to his refusal to let his athletic success be divorced from his life as a man. America wanted him to indulge their feelings about their city, team, and special events as a result of his success. They refused to acknowledge his accomplishments in favor of celebrating them on their terms. He refused to let them.

Only when bigotry forced his parents to leave his homeland of Monroe, Louisiana, far from their comfort and opportunities, did he become a member of an athletic family in Oakland, California. He attended McClymonds High School in West Oakland, also known as the "School of Champions," along with baseball Hall of Famer Frank Robinson. Curt Flood and Vada Pinson, who were both baseball All-Stars, attended the school as well. However, this is only possible because West Oakland was the area of the city where white city leaders forcibly relocated the vast majority of Black people in the 1940s.

Russell only moved to Boston, regarded as the most racist city in the United States, because neither the St. Louis Hawks' ownership nor their white fan base wanted a star Black player to represent the team. This included the legendary Bill Russell, who had just won gold for the United

States team at the 1956 Melbourne Olympic Games. Thus, the Hawks sent Russell, who had made his nation proud, to Boston in exchange for Ed Macauley and Cliff Hagan, two white players.

Russell reshaped the NBA, the Boston Celtics squad, and the NBA as a whole. Before Russell, the Celtics had never advanced to the NBA finals. The team belonged to the coach, Red Auerbach, and his star, Cousy. Cousy reveled in being the captain and the hero from the neighborhood college (Holy Cross), but he was unable to accept—as most great players are unable to—that a greater teammate was surpassing him in importance. With Russell, Cousy won six championships, but not one without him. Nine championships were won by Auerbach as a coach, while none were won by coaches after him.

The city reacted to the Celtics' success by failing to attract crowds, embarrassing Russell, and exposing racial discrimination by celebrating white players while only praising its Black ones whenever it could. At the University of San Francisco, Russell won two collegiate championships while feeling uneasy about the country's racial structure. He earned a gold medal for a nation whose Black children needed national guard protection to attend school in Little Rock, Arkansas, many months later.

Later that year, in 1957, Russell would win the NBA championship for a city with racial disparities so severe that by 1974, Boston would resemble Little Rock from 16 years earlier. Boston, at least in terms of reputation, hasn't recovered. Every step of Russell's professional career was shaped by American racism, and for years, many thought he was too resentful and couldn't get beyond the daily injustices that millions of Black people experienced. For years, he was judged not on what his country had done to him, but on the grounds of why he hadn't accepted it more graciously.

Sports are rife with meaningless clichés that lend the regular lives of talented players a heroic shine. They claim that iron sharpens iron. His response to Russell's calluses was winning at a tremendous pace. There are no superlatives, metrics, stats, generational comparisons, or period comparisons that can adequately describe a life lived, particularly one as ferociously outspoken and independent as Bill Russell's, since he refused to partake in the pomp while converting slights into domination.

When your Massachusetts house is broken into and covered in excrement, as Russell's once notoriously was, there is no measure for measuring the worth of victory, on finishing 21-0 in winner-take-all games throughout his last two years of college, the Olympics, and NBA. Even with all of his successes, it's likely that his greatest achievement was eliminating the distinction between human and athletic activities, which also made it difficult to see him without also seeing America. Russell took Birmingham, Selma, and MLK with him as he won eight consecutive championships, defeated the Lakers — always defeated them, never lost to them in the Finals.

It was impossible to enjoy the Celtics' victory against the 76ers without addressing the unfair treatment of him and his people. This was his unbreakable agreement. Russell made sure that one could not be evaluated without the other because he did not exist solely for the public's amusement, and as a result, it would be unethical to evaluate him without the public also taking a critical look at himself. For many years, the popular perception of Russell was that he was mired in the resentment of his day, although this wasn't quite the case. His reluctance to comply set him free. Despite being the coach of the Celtics in 1969, he was not there for either his entrance into the Hall of Fame or the team's last championship parade. Despite being far from the city where he gained popularity, he was always there.

When he wanted to be seen, he was – and throughout the latter 15 years of his life, he stood as a strong specter, as remote as his trademark chuckle. The MVP trophy for the NBA Finals was renamed in his honor. He was surrounded by the 2008 Celtics like a little child. For more than 50 years, he served as a living connection to the beginning of the game and the voice of activism, from Jackie Robinson to Colin Kaepernick. He was invisible when he didn't want to be noticed. Since 2013, there has been a statue of Bill Russell, much as there is one of Auerbach, one of Bird (at least his shoes), one of Williams, and one of Orr.

Russell will be the subject of many eulogies and reductive discussions in the days to come because, in the end, he was irreducible. eleven victories. Eight championships in a row. Regardless of the customarily high expense, he decided to stand firmly on his values and that it was not expensive to free himself from the pressure to work without regard. It wasn't Bill Russell who was caught; rather, his former community, city, and nation had to face their actions and attitudes and attempt to figure out why their greatest champion often avoided them.

Even Cousy attempted to make sense of his early handling of Russell, the period, and the Boston days decades later, more than half a century too late. He sent a letter to Russell.

Russell remained silent. Russell had grown beyond that long ago. It happened yesterday. Bill Russell was already free, whereas Cousy may still be troubled by all he chose not to say or do.

Chapter Three

Legacy of Bill Russell

Bill Russell enjoyed a life that is unmatched.

Russell was a really exceptional guy who had a lasting impression on the NBA and beyond, from his achievements on the basketball court to his much more significant contributions to society.

He is the greatest victor in the annals of American professional sports. He stood up to abuses while leading the Boston Celtics to their run of 11 titles in 13 seasons, and he was a fighter for civil rights. The NBA's Finals MVP trophy now bears his name, making him the league's first Black head coach and the player with the most titles won in the league's 75-year history.

But Russell's impact extends far beyond just being inscribed on a trophy. He is still regarded as one of basketball's early greats, more than 50 years after his last game.

Here are some stories that help to illustrate why Russell is so well-known in NBA history and why he will continue to be for as long as the league exists.

The Victory in the End

There are several ways to explain Russell's sway over the court. The most remarkable, though, comes from a different illustrious basketball personality, veteran Boston Globe writer Bob Ryan, who chronicled Russell's last several seasons with the Celtics:

Between his time at the University of San Francisco, the Olympics, and his tenure with the Celtics, Russell participated in 21 separate winner-take-all matches, including NCAA tournament single-elimination games, Olympic single-elimination matches, and NBA playoff series-deciding Games 5 and 7.

How did Russell do in those contests? A chilly 21-0.

Russell's squad never lost a game when the losing team had to leave. Russell stood out from everyone in the history of the sport due to his unmatched will to succeed, even Wilt Chamberlain, his biggest adversary.

No opponent existed who Russell would feel terrified by or inferior to. Because of this, he is still regarded as the greatest winner in American professional sports history more than 50 years later. Like many other aspects of Russell's life, it is difficult to fathom someone stealing this title from him.

Just consider it one last triumph for a guy who lived his life accumulating them at a historic rate.

Unknown Person in Alcatraz

Russell and the other four starters from the first college basketball dynasty sailed across San Francisco Bay to Alcatraz, the notorious island federal prison where mafia bosses, serial killers, bank robbers, and other violent criminals who the U.S. government thought couldn't be imprisoned elsewhere were kept.

Despite being informed that civilians weren't permitted there, Russell and his University of San Francisco teammates—winners of a record 55 straight games and two consecutive national championships—were granted unparalleled access to the prisoners. Why? The USF Dons, the first team to start three Black players (with Russell, future NBA Hall of Famer and Boston Celtic teammate K.C. Jones, and guard Hal Perry), were thought to be able to ease tensions between the prison's Black and white prisoners.

Russell, a 6-foot-9 guy dressed in a coat and tie and sporting a hat atop his head, made his way to his comrades beside Robert Stroud, the infamous "Birdman of Alcatraz," who was held apart from the other prisoners.

John Hernan, a former corrections officer who was there that day and walked the players through "Broadway," the major walkway between C and B blocks, once said, "In my time, I never saw any other civilians inside the [cellhouse]." They would be the only people who would go down Broadway as they did, now that you bring it up.

Russell, a USF player who averaged 20.6 points and 21 rebounds that season, was revered by the prisoners. His statistics were yelled at him. Carl Boldt, a USF teammate of Bill Russell's, said that "they looked at Bill Russell like he was God."

After more than 50 years, the Golden State Warriors established their own dynasty and surpassed Russell's Dons as the best basketball team to represent the Bay Area. His teams won the title in 18 of the 21 years he played, but by that point his career was in the rearview mirror, consigned to the annals of history. However, Russell, who grew up a few streets from Oracle Arena in Oakland, and his teammates were all too familiar with what it was like to be the talk of the Bay, to thrash opponents game after game, and to rejoice at the conclusion of the season. According to a person close to him, Russell would find a television and turn it on anytime the Warriors were playing.

The NBA Founding Father

In addition to all of his achievements, we should never forget Russell as the NBA's supreme senior statesman, our emeritus champion, who consistently contributed his unequaled gravitas to enhance the league's most significant ceremonies.

In this capacity, microphones caught their memorable exchange on the sidelines of the 2008 All-Star Game with Kobe Bryant.

Then Russell remarked, "See, I watch a lot of your games." "You know, when I watch your matches, I attempt to determine each player's objective and how well he is pursuing it. That's how I choose to view it. The reality is that I would be more proud of you if you were my own son."

These types of fatherly moments perfectly encapsulate the influence Russell had even after he stopped participating in sports and coaching. In his 80s, he elegantly assumed the role of the NBA's unofficial guru.

On paper, Russell had an unbeatable resume as a player, coach, and civil rights activist, but in reality, it was his amiable demeanor, his trademark smile, and his genuine concern for younger players that allowed him to thrive in his role as the patriarch of the great league he had helped legitimize as a player and coach decades earlier.

Former commissioner David Stern said in February 2009 that the NBA will honor Russell with the title of Finals MVP "Bill served as an example for a generation of Americans, not just basketball fans. He is revered by his coworkers, instructors, and fans, and it is obvious that his legacy has stood the test of time."

Russell devoted all 88 of his years to creating the greatest legacy this sport has ever known.

11 titles are won through defense.

Russell, more than any other NBA player, had a significant influence on basketball and the success of his club. And the data reflect that.

Every single one of his 11 victories may be attributed to Russell's hegemony.

Russell's Celtics often had below-average offenses as determined by team offensive rating, despite having all of his Hall of Fame colleagues. But the defenses—goodness, the defenses—are so important!

In 12 of Russell's 13 seasons, the Celtics' defense was the best in the NBA, sometimes by improbable margins. The Celtics' defensive rating in 1963–64 was a staggering 10.8 points per 100 possessions higher than the league average. The greatest offense that season, in contrast, barely outperformed the league average by 4.3 points per 100 possessions. Despite ranking last in the NBA in offensive rating that season, the Celtics won the title.

The Celtics' defensive rating in 1964–65 was 7.4 points per 100 possessions more than the club in second place. Once again, despite having one of the weakest offenses in the NBA, the Celtics won the chip.

That illustrious run, which had five of the top-25 measured defenses in history in five straight seasons at Russell's prime, began with his arrival in 1956. Russell's inaugural season saw the Celtics win the title with the greatest defense in the NBA, and in his 13th and last season, they repeated the feat.

The Celtics' defense fell to the lowest half of the league the season after Russell retired.

End Notes

The two greatest centers in the history of the sport were Bill Russell and Wilt Chamberlain.

Whoever you compare the two to or who you decide to choose, both centers have accomplished enough in their professional lives to qualify as the finest centers to ever play the position.

Whether Wilt, the scoring machine who had no trouble scoring 60 points or more.

Or there was Russell, the ideal teammate and rebounding magnet. Oh, and throughout his 13-year career, he also won 11 NBA Championships.

No one who has played with or against the two can dispute that Wilt was the most gifted of the two. Russell consistently provided his Celtics the greatest opportunity to win a championship.

Russell performed well in the postseason whereas Wilt excelled throughout the regular season.

Russell excelled in the stressful moments, while Wilt was nonexistent in critical or clutch situations.

In the 1961–1962 season, Wilt averaged 50 points per game, and Russell was awarded the league's Most Valuable Player.

For Wilt, the numbers—how many points or rebounds he scored—were everything. Simply put, Russell had an obsession with success and accolades.

Only what his detractors thought of him interested Chamberlain. Only what his teammates thought of him was important to Russell.

Wilt won two NBA championships. Russell took eleven.